S.M.A.R.T

Women

Manage Their Money

Tips for the *Girl Boss*

ALLISON DENISE ARNETT

DEDICATION

For the Do-It-Yourself (DIY) Creative Girl Boss who stepped out on faith to Be Purposeful, Get Paid, and Sit Pretty. I see you and I believe in you. May you discover the mindset and the methods required to start managing your business finances the SMART way.

CONTENTS

ACKNOWLEDGMENTS

Father God, thank You for the inspiration to inspire others. Thank You that my career experiences make it possible to teach others something valuable. May it be acceptable in Your sight.

One

WHO AM I TO TALK

It's not who you are that holds you back,

it's who you think you are not.

--Denis Waitley

Fellow Girl Boss

Simply put... I am you. I am the girl who knew there was more to life than a 9-to-5. I am the serial entrepreneur. I am the do it yourself creative. I am a fellow girl boss. We wear many hats. The fun hats like networking at mixers. And the not so fun ones like bookkeeping. BLAH! That word probably leaves a bad taste in your mouth lol. I get it. But in over 17 years of accounting experience, there's one thing I've come to learn: not liking something is not a good enough reason to not do it. Especially when it's necessary. Neither is not understanding a thing. They say knowledge is power. And "they" my girl boss friend, are right.

Change your mind

A big part of being a smart money manager starts with your mind set. Poor money mindset breeds poor money management. Changing your mind is not the easiest thing to do. So I'm here to help with that. The most effective method I have found for changing your thoughts is to cancel the negative thoughts and replace and reaffirm them with positives. Simple as that. With that said, at the end of each section you will find money mindset affirmations to serve as the glue between your thoughts and your actions. Read them. Repeat them. Internalize them. Believe them.

This is for you

- This is for you whether you choose to do your own bookkeeping or outsource it.
- This is for you if you still keep your business and personal finances in the same bank account.
- This is for you if you want to learn how to organize your financial data.
- This is for you if you are ready to take control of your business finances.
- This is for you if you want to learn the S.M.A.R.T way to manage your money.

Yes my pretty, this is for YOU. So, enough small talk. Let's dig in!

MONEY MINDSET AFFIRMATION

Every day I get better at managing my money.

Two

WHY MANAGING YOUR BIZ FINANCES IS IMPORTANT

important

adjective

of great significance or value; likely to have a profound effect on success, survival, or well being.[1]

Know how your business is doing

Your business is your baby. And what mom does not want to know how her baby is doing. You shed blood, sweat, and tears. You labored for months.

You put your mind and body through things you didn't know you could handle. All to birth this baby! And you mean to tell me that once it starts growing you're just going to leave it to its own devices? Or drop it off in someone's hands and leave it all up to them? Please say no. Businesses, like babies, need care and attention and, in my opinion, can sometimes be high maintenance. But, it's a labor of love. Running your business may be the hardest thing you ever do but it may also be the most rewarding. You owe it to yourself and your business to know how it's doing. How else can you care for it and nurture it into being all that you envisioned? Is it thirsty for income? Is it drained from expenses? Is it crying out for attention or is it thriving? These are only things you can know if you're paying attention.

Know where your money is going to and coming from

So you've been nurturing your baby and it's been growing. You're so proud of what it's becoming. It's almost taking on a life of its own. Maturing and making money. Maturity can be beautiful. It can also be trying. Kind of like a teenager. You question them when they're going out and you question them when they come back in. You may even keep tabs on them while they are out. Why? Because you know what happens when you don't keep tabs on them... they go buck wild! Why? Because where there is no structure there is no strength. Checking in is a form of protection... a form of care. This brings me to my next point. The same applies to your business.

Avoid fraud and theft

You may be in the business of coaching, graphic design, or some other fabulous service but there are some people who are in the business of taking what's yours without your permission... often slipping right under your nose. You may not be able to put them out of business but there are ways to protect yours. Staying on top of your business finances is one of those ways. Let me tell you a story: The story of a client who was not in the habit of managing their money on a regular basis. Let's call her Nina. Nina did the bare minimum. Checking to make sure she had money in her account but not so much checking the day to day transactions regularly. At year-end when it was time to prepare her bookkeeping for her tax return she found several unrecognizable electronic withdrawals from her account by a well-known company name. Come to find out it was fraud and because she discovered the fraudulent transactions months after they occurred the bank was unable to refund her hundreds of dollars. Now I don't know about you, but my coins are precious and I don't have hundreds of dollars to give to thieves. Moral of the story: you need to know where your money is going to and coming from.

Stay organized to be tax and audit ready

Tax time is crazy enough without you having to run around like a chicken with your head cut off because you can't find your documents or can't figure out how to pull all your financial data together. There's something to be said about having organized financial records and that is: "It pays." That's right it pays to be organized. How so? Taking organized financial data files to your

CPA or tax preparer saves you money. And you know what they say about a penny saved... it's a penny earned. Furthermore, having all your "bucks" in a row and your receipts in a file during an audit can keep money in your account. How so? Deductions of expenses that cannot be sufficiently proven can be taken away leaving you with penalties and interest to pay. I'm going to share with you some of my favorite tips for keeping your financial data organized. Let's go.

MONEY MINDSET AFFIRMATION

I understand the importance of managing my money.

Three

THE S.M.A.R.T. WAY TO MANAGE YOUR MONEY

Don't make excuses for why you can't get it done. Focus on all the reasons why you must make it happen.

-- Ralph Marston

So when it comes to managing your business finances there are certain key things that should be implemented by you whether you manage your money yourself and do your own bookkeeping or if you outsource and hire someone to do it for you.

Now you might be asking the obvious question which is, "why would I want to manage my money if I've hired someone else to do it for me? Doesn't that defeat the purpose of outsourcing?" And to that I remind you of our last lesson on importance: avoiding fraud and theft and knowing how your business is doing. Listen, embezzlement is real and so is the struggle of not knowing the financial health of your business. So when you read these next few points think of them from either frame of mind because I assure you they apply to you either way.

S.M.A.R.T

Scan and save business receipts and documents.

Why pay premium CPA or tax accountant hourly rates to do something that you can do for yourself in five seconds? Your smart phone is the first virtual assistant you'll ever have. Using your camera phone to snap pictures of your business receipts and documents saves you time, money, and headache. Even better are the various receipt scanning apps available that can automatically categorize your transactions and link it to your accounting software for you in the matter of seconds. We will go more into setting this up in the next chapter.

Make it a priority.

The principles in this book won't work unless you do. It's easy and tempting to say I'll get back to this later or I'm too busy. To that I say you can either make time now or you can make time later when you have to go back and clean up messes or search piles of papers for things you could have scanned and had readily available. Don't do double work. Just make it a priority to keep track of your finances now.

Ask questions and ask for help.

Reading and learning from this book is a form of asking. So you already know you have the willingness to ask what you don't know. Take advantage of the assets around you such as knowledgeable family and friends, groups you are a part of, or Google. Closed mouths don't get fed and no (wo)man is an island. The people who come to you for your expertise have learned to ask for help. When you ask for help you allow others to serve in their God-given purpose.

Revisit your financial status monthly.

A coin check should be done on a monthly basis. Take a hint from the banks. Don't you receive your bank statements at the end of every month? The banks are onto something here. Most statements, bills, invoices, etc are produced on a monthly basis. So pray tell: Why would you wait 12 months to look at your financial status? Hey Pretty, make a monthly date with your business to compare your data to your bank statement for accuracy and fraud. Trust me your business is a complete gentleman...it WILL pay the check.

Take advantage of the tools available to you.

Technology is more advanced than it's ever been and is steadily advancing. With that said, know that there are countless apps, software, and websites available at the touch of a finger. And get this:

some of them are free! So cut the excuses and find out what's available for what you need then use it.

MONEY MINDSET AFFIRMATION

I am taking the necessary actions to smartly manage my money.

Four

TAKE CONTROL TODAY:
3 ACTIONABLE STEPS

A year from now you may wish you had started today.

-- Karen Lamb

ACTION 1:

Open a separate bank account for your business

Different banks may have various requirements for

documents needed to start your business checking account. This is often determined by what legal form of business you have but what you can do today is choose.

Challenge:

Choose a Bank, see what's required, and start your new bank account in the next three days.

Choosing your new bank: NerdWallet.com has a great tool to help you select the best checking account. They also have a state-by-state comparison list you may find helpful. Some things to compare when selecting your new bank account are

- your location
- the bank's location
- monthly fees
- opening deposit
- interest earned (if any)
- minimum monthly balances
- transaction volume fees

See what's required: Typically you will need:

- a minimum deposit amount
- two forms of ID (usually at least one picture ID)
- Federal ID Number (FEIN) or Social Security Number (SSN) (for Sole Proprietors)
- Certificate of Assumed Name (DBA) for Sole Proprietors or your articles of formation for the corporations, LLCs, partnerships, etc.

ACTION 2:

Scan and save all business receipts and documents

Which app you choose to use for managing your receipts and documents is left to personal preference but keep in mind that life will be easier if it can sync with your accounting software. Two that I have used personally are Expensify and Shoeboxed. See my downloadable comparison chart for more info on each.

Select and download the receipt scanner of your

choice and make a mental note to scan the next business related receipt or document you receive.

ACTION 3:

Choose an accounting system and use it

Some accounting systems are more robust than others. Some are more user-friendly. Here are three to choose from: Wave Accounting, Fresh Books, and QuickBooks. See my downloadable comparison chart for more info on each. Then pick one, sign up for it, and start using it today.

Challenge:

Select and sign up for your new accounting software in the next seven days and start using it.

MONEY MINDSET AFFIRMATION

I accept these challenges and commit to getting them done because it is imperative to my success.

SEVEN DAY START SMART MONEY MANAGEMENT CHALLENGE

Day One:

Research and choose your business bank and determine their requirements.

Day Two:

Gather all required documents to open your account. This could include applying online for a FEIN.

Day Three:

Open your new business checking account. Then CELEBRATE!!!

Day Four:

Research and choose your accounting software.

Day Five:

Signup for and setup your new accounting software. Get familiar with it.

Day Six:

Research and choose your receipt scanning app of choice.

Day Seven:

Signup for, setup, and test your receipt scanning app. Then CELEBRATE!!!

ABOUT THE AUTHOR

You can find more info about me or working with me on my website:

www.imallisondenise.com

Also feel free to email me with questions:
Allison@ImAllisonDenise.com

Join a great community of Women Entrepreneurs like yourself to get more tips and accountability in my Facebook Group:

Purposeful, Paid, & Pretty

RESOURCES

To Select a Checking Account
http://www.nerdwallet.com/business-checking-accounts/

State-by-State Comparison List
http://www.nerdwallet.com/blog/banking/find-free-business-checking-account/

Smart Money Tools Comparison Download

www.thecreativeaccountant.com/smartwomenebook

FOOTNOTES

All company names mentioned are trademarks or registered trademarks of their respective holders. Use of them does not imply affiliation or endorsement by them.

"important." *Dictionary.com*. 2015. http://www.dictionary.com (27 November 2015).